T0381115

THE DANCE

THE POWER OF THE FATHER, PARENTING THROUGH DIVORCE AND SEPARATION, DON'T LET YOUR CHILDREN BECOME COLLATERAL DAMAGE

MARVA ANN JONES

BALBOA.PRESS
A DIVISION OF HAY HOUSE

Scripture quotations marked NIV are taken from the Holy Bible, New International Version®. NIV®. Copyright © 1973, 1978, 1984 by International Bible Society. Used by permission of Zondervan. All rights reserved. [Biblica]

Balboa Press books may be ordered through booksellers or by contacting:

Balboa Press
A Division of Hay House
1663 Liberty Drive
Bloomington, IN 47403
www.balboapress.com
844-682-1282

Because of the dynamic nature of the Internet, any web addresses or links contained in this book may have changed since publication and may no longer be valid. The views expressed in this work are solely those of the author and do not necessarily reflect the views of the publisher, and the publisher hereby disclaims any responsibility for them.

The author of this book does not dispense medical advice or prescribe the use of any technique as a form of treatment for physical, emotional, or medical problems without the advice of a physician, either directly or indirectly. The intent of the author is only to offer information of a general nature to help you in your quest for emotional and spiritual well-being. In the event you use any of the information in this book for yourself, which is your constitutional right, the author and the publisher assume no responsibility for your actions.

Any people depicted in stock imagery provided by Getty Images are models, and such images are being used for illustrative purposes only. Certain stock imagery © Getty Images.

Print information available on the last page.

ISBN: 979-8-7652-5387-8 (sc)
ISBN: 979-8-7652-5389-2 (hc)
ISBN: 979-8-7652-5388-5 (e)

Library of Congress Control Number: 2024914475

Balboa Press rev. date: 08/09/2024

CONTENTS

I want to express my gratitude to my parents, Eva M. Jones Powell and the late Marvin C. Jones, who loved, taught, protected, encouraged, and supported me. It was because of them being extraordinary people and parents that I was inspired to write this book. I am forever indebted to my parents. I thank my brothers, Terry W. Jones, and David C. Jones, who are not only my brothers but dear friends. As a child they walked me to the bus stop, taught me how to tie my shoes, and how to ride a bike. I thank God we have remained close and enjoy spending time together. To my sisters-in-love the late Tracy Lea Jones and Joan Holling, I appreciate our sisterhood and friendship. It is only because of the love, encouragement, and support of my family that I have been able to accomplish my goals.

To the most beautiful nieces and great-niece on the planet, Tiffani Jones, LaQuae Jones, and Aymia Jones, I am so proud and honored to be your aunt.

Many thanks to all my family; my extended family, The Joneses of Booneville, Mississippi and "the Trotter Fourteen".

I am grateful for the guidance of my uncle, Dr. Joe Trotter, and my aunt, the late H. LaRue Trotter, who believed in me to accomplish great things.

To my aunt the late Josie L. Harris who used to tell people "Marva is a genius" (that's so funny), my aunt the late Dee Pannell who told the best jokes, my Aunt Bobbie who attempts to call me first on every holiday, my Aunt Isalene who makes herself available for every special moment in my life, to my Aunt Doris for all of our heart to heart talks, that end and start again, with "one more thing", to my Aunt Voncille/Auntie Mom and her husband Uncle Mel, my prayer warriors, to "My Night Owl Crew," my Aunt Mecca/ my twin, my Aunt Jessie/Ms. Tickle-Tickle, and the baby of the Trotter 14 my Aunt Sakina who never misses the chance to celebrate the people she loves. Thanks to my Uncle John (Aunt Sakina's husband), who lovingly calls me, "Bishop."

To my uncle Rahmaan who is always doing "Rahmaan Things" including the sweet things, like remembering my favorite tea, and to his beautiful wife, my Aunt Winona that keeps him in check, to my Uncle Otis for his example of resolve and strength and to his lovely wife, my Aunt

Pam who demonstrates true love daily, and to my Uncle David who challenges me and provides me with words of encouragement, constantly.

A special thanks to my first cousins that grew up with my brothers and me more like siblings than cousins, Salena (Dale) Johnson, Darlene (Darrell) Johnson, Donnie (Regenia) Harris, Bruce (Carla) Harris, and Greg (Melissa) Harris. We shared secret handshakes, the love of music, and days of teaching your nerdy sister-cousin the latest dances. Thanks for the work you put into trying to make me "cool."

Also, I want to thank my true friends, who have encouraged me along the way. To my friends who have been on life's journey with me for over 35 years, Shelia McGhee, Yul McLaurin, Deidre Campbell, Stacy Ede, Jill Parham, Mary Jane Brooks, and the late Debbie Rolland Anderson; thank you for your friendship through the ups and downs.

A special tribute to Mr. and Mrs. Scott (Mary) Christian, the late Mr. and Mrs. Ernest (Betty) Brown, Marsha Malone, the late Linda Brown Cochran, and the late Saundra Mitchal my lifelong friends, that became family.

Honor and Admiration to my grandparents the late Joe W. Trotter, Sr. and the late Thelma O. Trotter; the late

Andrew "A.J.". Jones and the late Aimee Aline Jones. It is my prayer that I am a positive representation of their legacy.

To the Oliver Family, thank you for supporting me throughout the years and sharing my third set of grandparents with me, the late Moses Oliver and the late Birdine Oliver.

I want to thank my husband, Matt Lundy, who has been patient with my being home but not present countless hours, days, and nights while doing this important work. Thank you for standing with me so that I could answer this call on my life.

I am blessed to have a village. You have all richly blessed my life. I am looking forward to spending more time with all of you!

Last but certainly not least, I thank God for giving me the strength to persevere and the mind to write this book.

INTRODUCTION

This book is something that I have carried in my spirit for many years. The longer that I was in practice helping individuals, couples, and families, the more relevant and at times urgent I believed it was for me to complete this book. This book speaks about our changing family dynamic, the staggering divorce rate in our nation, and the number of children born into single-parent households or who end up in one because of a divorce.

To single parents, women or men, I admire you for your strength. If you are doing what is necessary to provide for your children and guide them through this life and world that is ever changing and challenging, thank you for being that parent your child or children can rely on and deserve. Remember to celebrate yourself on March 21, which was declared Single Parents' Day in 1984.

My perspective about the family and how God intended our families to be is in no way detracting from single mothers or fathers who are doing it on their own or are capable of parenting on their own. However, if we are honest with ourselves, we know that God has designed a divine order for the family. He never intended for any parent, mother or father to have to parent alone.

Many have questioned why a woman who has chosen not to be a mother would even attempt to tackle this topic of parenting through separation or divorce. My reason for addressing this issue is to help parents understand the importance of co-parenting effectively for the sake of their children.

I don't have the perspective of a parent, but I do have the perspective of a child of parents who had been married for twenty years and then decided to divorce. I can speak about my feelings, how the divorce impacted me personally, and what I still needed from my mother and my father. My brothers and I are some of the fortunate children of divorced parents because we had the comfort of knowing they both continued to love us regardless of the status of their relationship.

My childhood was wonderful. I am the youngest of three and the only girl. Our parents married young—my father was twenty-one and my mother was nineteen. This was in the

1950s. I didn't realize how young they were when they had the responsibility of working full-time jobs, being business owners and homeowners, and having three children ages four, two, and an infant (me).

My mom and dad with their firstborn, Terry

My dad and brothers getting ready to go to church

My brothers and me, left, David and right, Terry

Life seemed very simple for us as children. We had no idea about the work and sacrifice our parents were making to give us the best they could. We lived in a small town where all the neighbors knew one another, and of course none of the adults had a problem correcting children or making a quick phone call to their parents if necessary.

Without question I was a Daddy's girl, born the day after his birthday and named after him. His name was Marvin, and I am Marva. My parents knew how to parent together;

there was no pitting them against each other, they were in sync, and they truly appeared to me to be the perfect couple.

My mom and dad on their way to dance

They would work different shifts so that one parent was always at home. No strangers babysat us; it would always be a family member or someone in the neighborhood with whom we were familiar. My paternal grandmother relocated from Mississippi to Ohio when I was born to help my parents with their three children all under the age of five.

We were a church-going family. My father was a deacon in the church, and my mother was a Sunday school teacher. They were still under the age of thirty but seemingly had it all together, which amazes me now. At the time I didn't understand the magnitude of what they were doing; they were just Mom and Dad. I am sure that most children don't understand until they are adults themselves the level of responsibility and sacrifice that good parents make for the sake of their children.

I fondly remember them going on dates, getting all dressed up and going to cabarets, especially on New Year's Eve. They were known for being great dancers and even won dance contests—hence the title of this book, *The Dance.* Being in sync with each other is what is necessary to parent effectively whether you are married or not, but if you are separated or divorced, being in sync is even more crucial.

Our family life was great until it wasn't. Around the age of thirteen, I started to see a change in how my parents interacted with each other. Something was missing. The once-happy home now seemed tense. My oldest brother was a high school junior or senior by this time; at the age of seventeen he graduated and went into the Army. My brother David and I were still living in the home.

I will never forget the summer of 1977. I was fourteen going on fifteen, and David was seventeen. Our parents' relationship had deteriorated, and we all knew it. I remember grabbing each of my parents by the hand and telling them we needed to talk. I told them they needed to do something because school would be starting soon, and we needed to get back to the happy place in our home. They were so receptive, and I felt heard when I walked away, but I was not prepared for what was to come in the next few months. My parents sat down with David and me to let us know they were getting a divorce. I could not imagine how this impacted my oldest brother—to leave home with a family intact and then come back to a home where your father no longer resides.

This was not what I expected. I think I believed they would meet with the pastor, get counseling, something—but not get a divorce. My mind was full of all kinds of thoughts, mostly questions: *How did we get here? Was I to blame because I told them they needed to do something? Who is going to live where? Will I see both of my parents as much as I do now?*

Besides losing someone who had passed away, this was the most painful experience of my life. I started thinking about so many of the people I knew in the neighborhood, people I went to school with, and it was almost as if they had a meeting and decided that getting a divorce was suddenly *the thing* for the thirtyish and fortyish people to start doing. My fear stemmed from the fact that so many of my peers were losing contact with their fathers and their relationships were not the same; I couldn't bear the pain of that, not Daddy's girl.

My parents agreed on all the details, which allowed them to get a dissolution instead of a divorce. My mom said the judge asked her about writing an order for child support and visitation, and my mom's response was that it wasn't necessary because there was no way my dad wouldn't take care of his children or see them. They may not have ended up being the perfect couple, but they were in my mind the perfect parents; they co-parented seamlessly even after their marriage was over.

My father moved to a place within walking distance; for a short time, he moved in with his best friend, Mr. Brown, who was separated from his wife at the time, but The Browns eventually got back together. Within about six months, my dad purchased a house that was down the street and around the corner, still within walking or bike-riding distance. He and my mother would talk often. There were no secrets:

whatever we did with one parent, the other parent knew about it in a second. It was certainly a time of adjustment, even though they tried extremely hard to avoid things being too different for us.

The strangest part about that time of my life is that I don't remember moving day. My father must have moved while my brother and I were in school. I do remember coming home, checking the closets where my dad kept his clothes, and not seeing any remnants of him. His clothes were gone, his shoes were gone, the once-full drawers were empty, with no razors and no aftershave. This was the day of reality. This was happening.

Waking up and knowing that our father was no longer living in the home was difficult, but we made the best of it. At Christmas he would still buy our Christmas tree, he and Mom would both buy gifts, he would be there when we opened our gifts, and he would come by with groceries all the time. He was present as much as he could be.

Both of my parents went on with their individual lives, dating, remarrying, and divorcing again. Their dating histories are for another book, especially my father's. He was quite popular. However, one constant was that, as parents, they were solid. I imagine it may have been difficult to acclimatize to our nontraditional family that was still very much a family. If people were going to be in my father's life, they had to respect my mother; if they were going to be in my mother's life, they had to respect my father; and they had better not even think about mistreating their children.

Although life after divorce is different, it can still be good; my parents did their part to make that happen for us. Even once we were all grown up and on our own, they continued to co-parent. On special occasions such as graduations or birthdays, both of our parents would be there. They got along and, typically, worked together to plan special events.

The day I graduated with my master's, my parents showed up wearing the same color, still dancing!!!

One moment that stands out was a time I was sick and had to have surgery; I was thirty-two at the time. My father had retired by this time after working thirty-two years for the same employer; he was only fifty-one years old when he retired. After retiring he relocated to his home state of Mississippi, and even though we were all grown, that was so hard for me. However, he would come back to Ohio as if it were down the street and around the corner. The night before my surgery, I spent the night with my mother; then my father came to her house the morning of the surgery to pick us both up to go to the hospital. They both sat in the waiting room, an inseparable team when it came to their children no matter the age or the situation.

That is a gift that I want to share with the world: it is possible to parent children effectively even if the relationship between the parents doesn't last. Parenting can't stop. Every child deserves to have two parents who respect each other and provide their children with unconditional love. I will say that part of being able to do so is choosing well from the beginning. Be careful about whom you decide to have children with; my parents chose well. I feel I have the best mom in the world and had the best dad in the world until he went home to be with God on February 3, 2010.

My parents' dance stood the test of time!

CHAPTER 1

God's Divine Order for the Family

To begin this discussion, we must understand the following key terms: *power, father, mother, divine,* and *order.* I want to parallel the earthly and the heavenly father to illustrate the magnitude of God's power over the lives of His people and the role of an earthly father in his family.

Power is defined as "a possession of control, authority, or influence over others, ability to act or produce an effect, mental or moral efficacy, a source or means of supplying energy, the right to govern or rule, and compel obedience" (*Webster's Ninth New Collegiate Dictionary*).

Father is defined as "a man who has begotten a child, God the first person of the Trinity, Forefather, one related to another in a way suggesting that of a father to child, one that originates or institutes, source" (*Webster's Ninth New Collegiate Dictionary*).

The word (father) "has many figurative and derived uses; a spiritual ancestor (John 8:44, Rom 4:11), the originator of a mode of life (Gen 4:20), one who exhibits paternal kindness and wisdom to another (Judges 17:10), a revered superior (1 Sam 10-12; 1 John 2:13)" (*NIV Compact Dictionary of the Bible*).

Mother is defined as "a female parent, a woman in authority, the superior of a religious community of women, Source, Origin, maternal tenderness or affection, to give birth to, to give rise to, produce, to care for or protect like a mother." (*Webster's Ninth New Collegiate Dictionary*).

Divine is defined as "relating to or proceeding from God; supremely good, superb, and heavenly, Godlike." (*Webster's Ninth New Collegiate Dictionary*).

And finally, *order* (as a verb) is defined "to put in order, arrange, to give an order to, command, destine, ordain, command to go or come to a specified place, to bring about order, regulate, suggests a straightening out so as to eliminate confusion; *organize* implies arranging so that the whole aggregate works as a unit with each element having a proper function, a state of peace, freedom from confusion, and is harmonious." (*Webster's Ninth New Collegiate Dictionary*).

The heavenly Father is all knowing, and He has all power in His hands. It was by God that the heavens and the earth were created; because of His power, He was able to simply speak, and everything came into existence. Not only did everything come into existence, but it was good (*Holy Bible, King James Version, Genesis 1:1-24*).

Although God spoke and created creatures of the sea, of the sky, and the land—and saw that His creatures were good and then commanded them to be fruitful and multiply—it was not until He created man that He made a creature in His image. What a privilege and an honor. He did not stop there but then gave man rule over all that He had created. It was not until He made the man that the word *formed* was used in the text. God formed man from the dust of the ground. That means He took time to shape and mold the man in His likeness and image. (*Holy Bible, King James Version, Genesis 2:7*).

After forming the man known as Adam, He placed him in the beautiful garden of Eden and gave him specific instructions, including to not eat of the tree of knowledge of good and evil, and warned him that if he did, he would surely die. After that God set the divine order of the family.

He took one rib—not two or three but one rib—and created one woman, one wife for Adam, and they became one flesh. From the beginning of time, God saw fit to put a man and a woman together to create a family. (*Holy Bible, King Jame Version, Genesis 2:15*).

God could have continued to create from the dust, but He chose to create a man and a woman, and He provided them with instructions but also gave them free will. Has our free will gotten us so far off track that we no longer value the family? Strong, intact families make strong communities; strong communities make strong cities; strong cities make strong states; and strong states make strong nations.

I examine the ultimate Father–Child relationship (that's God and Jesus). He was born of a woman but was conceived by the Holy Ghost and was the only man of perfection to ever walk the earth. Jesus was obedient to the Father, and the Father was ever present with the Son. God gave the Son guidance every day; He was constantly in conversation with the Son. The Son knew He could depend on the Father, which gave Him strength to complete the will of God. He was tempted by the enemy three times but was unwavering in His faith and His obedience to His Father, the Almighty. The Father–Son bond gave the Son power, authority, and divine dominion. Their connection allowed the Son to work miracles, prophesy, and carry out His purpose to be the Savior of the world. Through it all, His Father was with Him.

If fathers remained connected to their children, what kind of impact would that have on the lives of children today? What kind of impact would that connection have on our world today?

I am not negating the importance of mothers in the lives of their children. In the world today, if there is one parent present in the life of a child, it is typically the mother. The fathers are at times absent due to children being born out of wedlock, the parents' breaking off a relationship or getting divorced, or perhaps the two parents never identified as a couple. No child is a mistake—all are born because God has a purpose for them.

Men and women are obviously made differently and bring different but equally valuable assets in the rearing of children. God is all encompassing, yet He still saw fit to provide His Son with an earthly mother and father. The mother is typically the nurturer and caregiver; the father often is the provider and disciplinarian.

The role of the father is so important that his children are to take his last name and are considered his seed. It is the father who determines the sex of a child, but the mother carries the child and brings forth life from her womb. It is the father who is to leave an inheritance to his children, according to the Word of God. The child's connection to his or her father is imperative to the child's development and to the child's having a clear understanding of his or her purpose. The disconnection between father and child is detrimental, as we will discuss in the following chapters of this book. Having a connection with both parents helps children develop a complete understanding of who they are. The connection to both parents also allows children to have the benefit of knowing all aspects of their culture and having a sense of identity.

The family is the primary way to transfer values in most cultures. Due to parents having less time in the home and mothers' working outside the home, about 60 percent of three- to- four-year-old children spend their days in day care, as compared to only 5.7 percent in day cares in 1965. Therefore, children are not learning their values from home but from outside the family, from babysitters, schools, and the media. Single-parent households further decrease the amount of family influence on children today. In addition, we have fewer children connected to their grandparents and other relatives due to nuclear families often being uprooted to pursue careers and education, which further contributes to values not being learned from the family (*Blackwell, Miniard, and Engel, 2001*).

It was truly a blessing for me to get to know and love my grandmothers, spend time with them, learn family history, and hear funny stories about my parents, aunts, and uncles when they were growing up. Unfortunately; both my maternal and paternal grandfathers passed away before I was born.

Children need and want the attention of both their parents and quite often will do whatever it takes to get that attention. If children cannot gain the attention by doing good deeds, they will resort to negative behavior. In the eyes of most children, any attention is better than no attention at all. How much has parental discord, single-parent households, and neglect of children accounted for the problems and the struggles that we see children and young adults facing today?

Parental discord and divorce are often to blame for children becoming disconnected from their fathers. Divorce causes significant problems for all involved, including the children, but they receive very little support in making their transition. The adjustment of the children is dependent on the events that follow the divorce and how the parents themselves handle those events (Clapp 1988).

Despite the traumatic effects of divorce, according to the US Census Bureau (2022) there were 2,015,603 marriages in 2019 and 746,971divorces—approximately 37 percent. (According to the publication the number of divorces excludes data for California, Hawaii, Indiana, Minnesota, and New Mexico) Although this rate shows a decrease from prior recent years, according to the Center for Disease (2021), the marriage rate also decreased. The divorce rate of second marriages is approximately 60–67 percent. In the US, divorces from 2000 to 2019 numbered 8.3 million.

On a scale of stressful life events, divorce ranks second only to the death of a spouse. Divorced people are six times more likely to be hospitalized for psychological disorders and have twice the rate of suicide as married people (Carter and McGoldrick 1988). According to a release from the US Census Bureau on November 17, 2022, concerning living arrangements of American families, there were 10.9 million single-parent family groups with a child under the age of eighteen, with 80 percent maintained by the mother. Further, a release by Pew Research on December 12, 2019, documents the United States having the world's highest rate of children living in single-parent households, with almost 25 percent of US children in one-parent households, which is more than three times the percentage of single-parent households around the world, at 7 percent.

There are countless negative impacts of divorce and children not having the privilege of both parents in their lives, which will be addressed in later chapters. However, I would like to focus the next chapter of this book on how to work toward maintaining marriages, keeping your family intact, and if divorce is the only way, how to do that with as little impact on your children as possible.

CHAPTER 2

Before I Let Go

One of the most important things when evaluating your relationship with your spouse is to not allow the opinions of family or friends to sway your decision on whether you choose to fight for your marriage or to let go. When we allow others to be a part of our decision-making process, pride can often become the reason for leaving the marriage without making every effort to reconcile.

Sometimes people share events that have occurred in their marriages with well-meaning family members and friends only to get the response, "If I were you, I would leave him or her." The combination of hurt and pride can lead to decisions that may not be in your best interest or that of your family long term.

Make sure you consider everything before you let go:

- How long have you and your spouse been together?
- Do you value the life that you have built together?
- Why did you fall in love with your spouse in the first place?
- Are you allowing one moment in time to erase years of a good marriage?
- How do you move forward from here?
- Are you truly over your husband or wife?
- Remember that you do not get to dictate your spouse's dating life or who they might marry next.
- You need to consider how you may feel about other men or women being around your children.
- Are you truly ready for what it means to be done?
- You may not have a relationship where you can visit the children whenever you want to. How will you establish visitation?
- How will you approach being at an extracurricular event to support your child?
- How will you celebrate your children's birthdays and holidays?
- What are you doing to explore your feelings to be sure that you are healing?

To move toward divorce when you have children, you must be ready to own and release your feelings to heal so that your feelings do not hinder your ability to co-parent. This issue will be addressed more in a later chapter.

Often infidelity leads couples to get a divorce. Although infidelity is difficult to work through, it is not impossible. Some people think they have found someone better than their spouses because, after they have told these "better people" everything wrong with their spouses, it is easy for those people to portray themselves as what the married people want, at least for a time.

In my practice, I often take a letter-size piece of paper, put a dot in the middle, and tell the couple in counseling, "The piece of paper represents your marriage; the dot represents the one thing that has happened that may have been hurtful. But one dot cannot define your entire life together unless you allow it to."

Sometimes distance in the marriage occurs. Both husband and wife are working full-time jobs; have two, three, four, five, or more children; are running a household; and are not taking the time to be intentional about spending time together to nurture their relationship. Always remember that your spouse needs to be dated, flirted with, talked to, listened to, hugged, and kissed, among other things.

Communication is key in any relationship; lack of effective communication will destroy a marriage. The most important aspect of communication to me is to make sure that it is respectful. Even when there are disagreements, attack the problem but not each other. Resorting to name calling is never appropriate, yelling is senseless because no one is listening anymore, and saying things you do not mean to inflict pain on your spouse because you are upset or hurt about something is never helpful.

I equate poor communication to watching someone cook your favorite meal while you sit in the kitchen, anticipating how good it is going to taste. It smells good, and looks good, and then you watch the person who prepared it walk over to the garbage can, take the lid off, and place your favorite meal on the garbage can lid. How likely are you to eat it? Probably not very likely because the presentation ruined it for you. Now imagine that the person finished cooking your favorite meal, went to the cabinet, got out their best piece of china, and put the meal on it. How likely are you to eat it? Probably very likely. The only thing that changed was the presentation.

Presentation is everything. We often speak our truth, but how we present it will determine whether people are willing to listen. A great message can be ruined by the wrong tone, yelling, and hurling insults, and the true message gets lost because of poor presentation. Don't serve your spouse words on a garbage can lid; use china if you want to be heard.

Identify the problem areas in your marriage and explore possible options to fix them before you let go. Seek counseling to get another perspective and to help you work through issues that you may not even recognize are causing marital conflict, such as having very different families of origin, not knowing how to manage disagreements, or holding on to past transgressions, which leads to unforgiveness and resentment.

Regardless of the decision you make for your relationship—whether you work on your marriage or proceed with a divorce—if you have children together, you are connected to each other for the rest of your lives. This connection does not have to be negative. It can be positive if you remember that you chose each other to be partners and to be parents together. That should always be a relationship that is one of love and respect, even if you are no longer in love with each other.

So, if you feel that divorce is still your choice, I want to share some important rules and tools to live by so that you and your co-parent can accept that your marriage has ended but your relationship continues.

Five important issues must be addressed: 1) owning and releasing your feelings to heal; 2) your relationship versus your child's relationship with your ex; 3) providing a safe space for children to process their feelings related to the divorce; 4) the dating game; and 5) untraditional family but still a family.

CHAPTER 3

Owning and Releasing Your Feelings to Heal

Divorce is a major life event to which it takes time to adjust. You cannot go through the process of dating, fall in love with someone, decide to get married, make plans together, buy a home together, build a life together, and most importantly have children together and then walk away without experiencing some emotions. Ignoring your feelings is the worst thing you can do because, if you do not allow yourself to explore and identify your feelings, they will come out in ways that are unhealthy.

A lot of the time, couples point the finger at each other as to why the relationship did not work. The reality is that each person plays a role in making a relationship work or not work. If you are angry, explore the emotions that are causing that anger: "I am angry because I feel betrayed, disrespected, unappreciated, abandoned" and the list goes on and on. Working through the feelings that you have concerning your marriage ending is essential to being able to effectively co-parent.

Make sure that your feelings do not interfere with communicating necessary information to the noncustodial parent. The term *noncustodial parent* is foreign to me; my parents never spoke in a way that discounted the relevance of the other parent's role in my life. However, when people do not take on their responsibilities and embrace their roles as parents, laws and rules are put in place to help them do that. It should never be the responsibility of a judge to help people parent their children; this should be something that every parent wants to do.

Although your feelings are important, they cannot be placed above your willingness to co-parent. There should be a policy to contact each other when important issues happen with your children, and you should have a conversation at least weekly just as a check-in to make sure that the two of you are staying on the same page with rearing your children.

You are still parents; the children should not have to miss out on the benefits of having a mom and a dad because the two of you decided to end your relationship or marriage.

Your children need to be at the center of your relationship. If you have not gotten to a place where you, at a minimum, like each other, love your children enough to be respectful toward each other. Choosing not to be involved in your child's life because you are no longer in a relationship or marriage is not punishment for your ex but is a punishment for your child and will have a negative impact on your child's well-being. Children of parents who have decided not to be together anymore should not be collateral damage of that decision.

A divorce entails more than the end of a relationship or marriage; it is the loss of all the things you had planned. It is coming to the acceptance that the person you thought you would grow old with is no longer your wife or husband. It is accepting that a person you may have come home to for the past several years will not be there for you when you get home from work anymore. It is accepting that every day of your life will be different, and you must allow yourself to grieve what has been lost.

Research notes that the best predictor to a child's adjustment to divorce is a healthy relationship with both parents. The child's ability to create or maintain a healthy relationship with both parents is determined by how well the parents adjust to the divorce. Parents who do not adjust well can become bitter and resentful and say negative things about the other parent, which negatively impacts the child.

The relationship with the noncustodial parent, usually the father, is most vulnerable. An article in the *Tampa Bay Times* originally published February 7, 1996, stated that nearly 40 percent of fathers no longer have contact with their children one year after divorce.

Some fathers feel depressed and have a sense of loss but find it difficult to overcome the barriers to restore their relationships with their children following a divorce. Other fathers find it easy to withdraw, which is evident in how they do not visit their children or pay child support (Clapp, 1988). This may be due to the ongoing parental conflict, so, to avoid the conflict, the noncustodial parent withdraws totally. The custodial parent, usually the mother, may insist on the child's allegiance to her and feel threatened by a stable parent-child relationship with the noncustodial parent.

If you fail to own your feelings and work through them, you will live a lifetime harboring unforgiveness and resentment, which will keep you from enjoying your life. Be honest with yourself; don't try to act as if divorcing or ending a significant relationship doesn't have an impact on you.

Granted, there are times when people have made poor choices that led to a child being born; but having that child is no mistake, and the child is not a mistake but is here because God has a plan for him or her. Your responsibility is to accept the blessing and be the best parents possible.

CHAPTER 4

My Relationship with My Ex versus My Child's

Contrary to what you may believe, this process is not about you but about your children. Your children are not to be used as pawns so that you and your ex can harass each other, gain control over each other, or interfere in each other's potential new relationships to make each other miserable because you have chosen to be miserable. You and your children, believe it or not, are not a package deal, so you as the custodial parent cannot keep the child or children away from the other parent because you have not worked through your issues and now want to control how much, if at all, the children will see the other parent.

If you haven't grown up yet, it is time to grow up now. Your children are counting on both of you to be the parents they need you to be.

We unfortunately live in a world where people can be all consuming. Once you are a parent, your minor children's needs should always come before yours. Because someone didn't make a good partner for you doesn't mean that they are a bad parent. Allow your children to have their own relationships with their mother or father; it is not up to you to define the relationship your children have with the other parent. You may not like the other parent anymore, but your children likely love them. Don't try to turn your children against the other parent; they do not need to know what led to your divorce or separation.

I am so grateful that my parents did not talk negatively about each other. My parents never referred to each other as *ex-wife* or *ex-husband*; they always said "my children's mother" and "my children's father."

I am aware that hurtful things happen in marriage—some at the time seem unforgiveable—but if your children's other parent does not pose a threat to your safety or your children's safety, don't interfere with their relationship. Encourage them to have a relationship with the other parent; this is the person who will help you rear your children.

Don't allow friends to talk negatively about men or women in the presence of your children. Your sons do not need to hear their mothers talk about how awful men are. Remember, your boys will be men one day. And fathers should not talk about how awful women are. Your girls will be women one day.

Allow the children to call the noncustodial parent whenever they want to. If they are young and cannot do that without your assistance, help them. If they ask about the other parent, don't act annoyed. You may not want to have a relationship with them anymore, but your children need and want that relationship.

Your children may be excited about a fun time they had with the other parent and want to share that with you. Embrace that. Don't make your children feel that it is negative to have fun with the other parent; that is something you should be happy about. Every parent should want their children to have a happy and healthy relationship with both parents.

I remember spending nights at my dad's house. Our family has always been full of big sports fans, and on Friday nights, we would watch NBA games until we fell asleep. My father had been an outstanding basketball player in his day; one of my best memories was going to watch him play when I was a little girl. Then to see him transition from a player to a coach. I would walk in the gym as if my dad were playing in the NBA. I could share memories about my dad or talk about my weekend, and my mom would always be glad that I enjoyed time with my dad.

My brothers and I could also talk about our mom without our father being upset. If it was something funny, it would usually lead to one of them calling the other, talking about it some more, and laughing about it.

We were never questioned or interrogated about the other parent or what happened during a visit or an outing. There was just open conversation that seemed easy and natural.

If you are having difficulty separating your relationship with your ex from your child's relationship with their mother or father, seek counseling to work through your emotions and get to a place of healing and wholeness.

CHAPTER 5

The Dating Game

One of the most challenging things in ending a marriage or a relationship when you have children is that there will be a time when each of you will move on. You may be tempted to get angry because it may appear your former spouse has evolved into everything that you wanted them to be but with their new partner. You cannot react out of anger. Stay focused on parenting; that is now your role together, co-parents and co-parents only. The decision was made to end the relationship, and both of you must accept the next phase of your lives as single people. And single people date.

My caution to parents when dating is not to introduce everyone you decide to go out with to your children. Your children do not need to meet everyone you find to be cute, attractive, or interesting. Make sure that you get to know people well before you allow them to meet your children. It is a privilege to meet your children, and it is a very serious step that shouldn't be taken lightly.

Make sure your children understand that there can never be a replacement for their mother or father. Have a conversation with them about dating, see if they have questions, and allow them to openly share their thoughts and feelings.

There should be enough mutual respect between you and your former spouse that you will introduce your new mate to the other parent if things are getting serious enough that you want to introduce your new mate to the children.

Your new mate should not be trusted early in the relationship to be a babysitter for your children, especially children who are too young to tell you if something happened that was inappropriate. If someone is not treating your children well, they are not treating you well; exit the relationship immediately. Make good choices. Know the character of the person you are bringing into your life and the lives of your children. Having someone in your life who mistreats you is your choice, but don't put your children in that situation. Hopefully, you think enough of yourself to avoid unhealthy relationships.

Healing from your divorce or breakup is a must before

dating, and it takes time. Make sure you have worked through the feelings that came with ending your marriage. Take time to explore what you are looking for before you get into a new relationship. I refer to getting into a relationship too soon after ending a long-term relationship as "the bandage effect." You have a gaping wound that needs sutures, but you just put a bandage on it and keep going without getting the proper care for your wound. Bandages don't work for gaping wounds; starting a relationship before you have healed from a prior relationship doesn't work either.

If you want to simply date and not be in a committed relationship, don't introduce people you are casually dating to your children. It is unnecessary, unhealthy, and unfair to them. You might be confused, but that is no reason to confuse your children.

CHAPTER 6

Untraditional Family Dynamic but Still a Family

Make sure that you are clear about your family with anyone you date. You have children, and their other parent remains an important part of your children's life and yours. If you meet someone who cannot understand the dynamics of your family and wants to interfere in how you define your family, that is a person who is not mature enough to be in a relationship with someone who has children. If you have made the mature choice to have a positive, effective co-parenting relationship with your ex for the well-being of your children, make sure you do not forfeit that to date someone.

My parents were very clear with anyone they dated about our family dynamic, the mutual respect they had for each other, and the importance of continuing to parent their children regardless of the status of their relationship. Anyone who could not accept our family dynamic wasn't around very long.

It was challenging for many to accept our family because we remained close, which most people probably didn't understand. Some families with whom we had been longtime friends also went through divorces, but their families did not look like our family. Fathers were not as engaged with their children as my dad was with us. So, yes, we were unique.

Many years after my parents were divorced, my father was celebrating his seventieth birthday while living in his home state of Mississippi. He called my mother, told her that he was having a party for his birthday, and said he wanted all his family there and that included her. So, my mother made the trip with my brothers, their significant others, my two nieces, and me. We were all there to celebrate my father's seventieth birthday and my birthday, which was the day after his.

I loved that our family could spend time together without any issues. Even when both of my parents were remarried, we could all get together. Everyone at least played nice. I am not sure how it must have felt to be the spouses of my parents, but if anyone wanted a chance of staying around, they had to at least play nice.

Nothing, no circumstance, would ever separate the "Fab Five." We were inseparable. We were not a traditional family anymore but still a family. We had our struggles and went through difficulties, but no matter what the issue was, our parents were always there as a united front to support us.

Having pictures for special occasions with both of my parents is priceless. I have pictures following each of my graduations—with my high school diploma, my associate's degree, my bachelor's, my master's, and my PhD—and yes, from my wedding. Both of my parents were in attendance to celebrate their baby. The same goes for my brothers; whatever we were doing, our parents were there to support us. And of course, they were able to sit together.

My wedding photo at age thirty-four with both of my parents;
my dad was keeping his eyes on his new son-in-law

One of the most heart-breaking things I witnessed was when I attended a wedding. It was time for the parents of the bride to take photos with their daughter. The bride's father refused to take a photo with her and her mother because they were divorced, and he was remarried. I will never forget what a painful moment that was for the bride. She was so hurt. She and her husband had the most beautiful wedding except for that one unnecessary situation.

I want every child of divorced parents to have the experience that my brothers and I had. It seems so unfair that parents are not able to let go of their differences for the sake of their children. My parents could have chosen to hold grudges, but whom does that serve? No one. They were selfless, put aside their hurt feelings, talked some things through, forgave each other, and continued being the parents we needed and deserved.

My passion in life is to help as many people as possible save their marriages, but if they cannot work things out as a couple, I want to teach them how to co-parent effectively so that their children do not have to suffer because of their decision.

CHAPTER 7

The Divorce Aftermath for Adults and Children

Divorce is hurtful and a major adjustment not only for the couple but also for the children. According to the US Census Bureau data for 2009–2011, fatherless homes are linked to 63 percent of youth suicide, 90 percent of homeless or runaway children, 85 percent of children who exhibit behavioral disorders, 71 percent of high school dropouts, more than 50 percent of youths in prison, and over 50 percent of teen mothers. Some of the disruptive side effects in the lives of children of a divorce or breakup are loss of security and well-being, poverty, life with a parent and a live-in-lover, the remarriage of one or both parents, life in one stepparent family combined with visits to another stepparent family, and the breakup of one or both stepparent families.

There are documented long-term consequences of divorce for children. The severity of a child's reaction at the time of the divorce may not be a predictor of how the child will fare ten to fifteen years later. Boys have a tendency to initially show more anger than girls. I attribute this to a society in which boys and girls are treated differently. If a five-year-old girl is outside playing, falls and skins her knee, and runs into the house sobbing, she gets picked up, held, and comforted with reassurances that everything will be OK. However, if a five-year-old boy is outside playing, falls and skins his knee, and runs into the house sobbing, he gets told, "You are all right. Shake it off. Boys don't cry." So, boys learn at an early age that showing that they are hurt by crying isn't acceptable, and they soon show the emotion that society is comfortable with them showing, which is anger. That is true until he is about fifteen, when it becomes problematic.

In addition, the census data showed that boys between the ages of nineteen and twenty-nine were unhappy, were lonely, and had few lasting relationships with young women. However, researchers, Wallerstein and Blakeslee (1980) have found that the "sleeper effects" can affect two thirds of the girls in young adulthood, known as "feared betrayal and abandonment" by a man. Both sexes indicated they would live with a partner before marriage to avoid making their parents' mistakes (Clapp, 1988).

Even though my father remained active in my life, trusting in relationships and thinking about getting married were challenging for me. I was of the belief that, if my parents' marriage could end in divorce, I didn't have much hope of having a successful relationship.

The first year following the divorce is often filled with a lot of conflict; it often resembles the marriage but now the divorced couple is still finding something to argue about. The conflicts of divorced couples typically are about child support, visitation, or having different parenting styles. It is unfair for children to be at the center of parents' inability to be amicable and make decisions together for the benefit of their children.

Clapp cited two comprehensive and longitudinal studies conducted by Hetherington, Cox & Cox (1976, 1978a, 1985); and Wallerstein & Kelly (1983, 1984, 1985a, b, 1987) that indicated following a divorce, children receive less attention, less affection, less support, less communication, and erratic discipline. Older children feel neglected, while younger children fear abandonment. Children of divorced parents initially feel anxious, fearful, depressed, guilty, rejected, lonely, and angry, and they yearn for the missing parent, most often the father. They often fantasize about parent reconciliation (Clapp, 1988). These feelings are accompanied by difficulties in schoolwork and behavioral problems.

I personally can relate to feeling anxious, fearful, and guilty. Anytime a person is facing an unknown or uncharted territory, anxiety is a normal feeling. I recall being worried and afraid about staying close to my father when my parents divorced. I was daddy's girl and could not fathom that relationship changing. Thank God, my father made sure that he remained engaged with us, and we always knew he was there for us in every way—just as our mother was always there for us in every way. It was truly a blessing.

My feelings of guilt were related to my telling my parents that they needed to do something because they were obviously not getting along. I know now that their decision to divorce was not because of anything I said or did but because they took an honest look at their relationship. However, now as a therapist, I truly believe they loved each other enough that, with the right guidance, their marriage could have survived anything. Perhaps that is the little girl in me who will always wish that my parents had found a way to stay married and be happy.

I was always a good student, made the honor roll, and was the student of the month often. However, during the first quarter of my freshman year, I had the worst grades of my life. That was the year my parents divorced, and focusing on schoolwork was something I simply couldn't do. It was important to me for my parents to be proud of me, so I quickly regrouped and made the honor roll the next quarter. By that time, I was able to see that my dad was just as involved as he always had been, so my anxiety and fear dissipated.

According to studies, parent-child relationships seem to be in recovery after the second year of divorce; however, those relationships tend to have more conflict than in intact families (Clapp 1988). Some research suggests that some long-term problems result from divorce. Evidence suggests that boys living in divorced-mother-headed households tend to be more aggressive, impulsive, and rebellious than boys from intact families (Clapp, 1988). And according to Myers (2002), aggressive behavior is difficult to modify once the behavior is established.

For girls, the problems become more evident during adolescence, in heterosexual relationships. Quite often girls struggle with relating to men and boys due to the limited interaction with their fathers. While in social situations with boys or men, girls of divorced parents typically were more anxious, more attention seeking, inappropriately assertive, and more provocative than were girls from nuclear families. In addition, these girls married younger, became pregnant prior to marriage more often, and when they did marry, often married men who were immature, poorly educated with unstable employment, and tended to be hostile toward them and their children (Clapp 1988).

It was noted that the best predictor of a child's adjustment to divorce is a healthy relationship with both parents. The relationship with the noncustodial parent, usually the father, is the most vulnerable. In approximately 50 percent of divorces, children are estranged from their fathers and have no contact. Some fathers feel depressed and have a sense of loss but find overcoming the barriers to restore their relationships with their children following a divorce to be difficult. Other fathers find it easy to withdraw, which is evident in that they do not visit their children or pay child support (Clapp 1988). This may be due to the ongoing parental conflict; to avoid the conflict, the noncustodial parent withdraws totally. The custodial parent, usually the mother, may insist on a child's allegiance to her and feel threatened by a stable parent-child relationship with the noncustodial parent.

In a study conducted by Hingst (1981) that was cited by (Clapp 1988), 50 percent of children surveyed following the divorce of their parents indicated that the most distressing aspect of the divorce was missing their fathers, and 77 percent wished for more time with their fathers. Low self-esteem was a common thread among these children (Clapp 1988). Although the father-child relationship is instrumental for both girls and boys, studies have shown that boys have a more difficult time adjusting after a divorce. Further, a study referenced by (Clapp 1988) that was conducted by Santrock and his colleagues in 1982 indicated "that boys in the custody of their fathers following a divorce are more mature, independent, and sociable and less demanding than boys in the custody of their mothers." Girls tend to fare better in the custody of their mothers but still show signs of maladjustment as noted in this book.

Once the decision to divorce is made, it is crucial for the children's adjustment that parents make every effort to accomplish the following:

1. Put the best interest and well-being of the children first!

2. Be cordial with each other, avoid conflict, and implement healthy communication to address any parenting issues; demonstrate mutual respect.

3. Encourage children to express their feelings about the divorce or separation in a safe, loving, supportive, and nonjudgmental environment.

As a product of a divorced household, seeing my needs put first restored my sense of security in knowing that I did not have to choose between my parents and that both would be there for me. Seeing them get along gave me a sense of peace and decreased my level of anxiety. At that time, I didn't know what to call what I was feeling; I just knew that what I was feeling didn't feel good. It was as if someone had died—the life I had known for fifteen years was over, and I was unsure of what to expect. Even though my dad lived close by, it was still different not having him in the home. Now I realize that what I was experiencing was grief. It seemed that I should have been able to say something or do something that would make my parents want to stay together or get back together but, of course, be better than they were at the end of their marriage.

As stated throughout this book, my parents were able to become friends and, as a result, were an awesome team when it came to parenting. They chose not to set up child support or visitation through the court. My father paid the child support directly to my mother, and he could visit anytime he wanted to visit—and believe me, he did just that. Since my father purchased a house within walking distance from the family home, my parents worked out a schedule for cooking dinner and making sure that my brother and I got to and from school and extracurricular events (my eldest brother was in the Army when our parents divorced). All three of us had our challenges with adjusting, but I would imagine that having your parents married when you left home for the military and then returning home for leave to a single-parent household had to be a culture shock. My brother David and I had an opportunity to adjust by being there through the entire process, but Terry did not have that time to adjust.

Our family's situation was quite unique and special. Even as an adult child, I cannot express the importance of parents' being friends or at least cordial. My brothers and I did not have to decide which parent to invite for the holidays, birthday celebrations, or cookouts.

During the time of my parents' divorce, many of my peers' parents were divorcing as well. It was as if there was something in the air and divorce was the newest fad. It was sad to see what was happening to all these families.

On the other hand, we have all heard and seen news stories about situations much more devastating than divorce. There are times when divorce is the best option. When I see the devastation on the news of some families, it makes me feel blessed that my parents walked away from each other and were able to have mutual respect.

My family having a spiritual connection was another force that allowed my parents to be friends and helped to ground me personally. Trust me, I did a lot of the dumb stuff most teenagers do; but at the same time, I was a nerd and a bookworm and certainly had a vision of being successful. I have experienced the power of my earthly father and my heavenly Father in my life. Returning to our spiritual foundation will help to heal our families.

CHAPTER 8

Increase in Number of Children Being Diagnosed with Mood and Personality Disorders

With the increase of marital discord, single-parent households, and often absentee fathers also comes the increase of diagnoses given to children for a multitude of mood and personality disorders. When diagnosing any person, childhood experiences are relevant, but when diagnosing children, they become even more relevant because they are still living in the family environment. Based on research findings and my own personal experience with working with children, they are often impacted by their living environments to the point that their "dysfunction" is not their dysfunction at all but the dysfunction of their families, which causes the children to display characteristics of mood and personality disorders.

The diagnoses that will be reviewed in this book will illustrate that the behavioral patterns of children who have the various disorders are similar in nature to the behavioral patterns of children of divorced or unwed parents. In addition, many of these children are without a paternal relationship and therefore without paternal guidance. Yet this well-known fact has not stopped the continued diagnosing of our children, not to mention the medication that is being dispensed to them.

The status of the family is a pertinent component in the diagnosis and treatment of children. One of the assessments of the family environment is the Family Environment Scale, also known as the FES. The FES consists of ninety true-false items to assess the family's basic characteristics. The assessment has ten subscales to evaluate the cohesiveness, expressiveness, conflict, independence, achievement orientation, intellectual-cultural orientation, active-recreational orientation, moral-religious emphasis, organization, and control of the family unit. Further, the FES has three higher-order factors: supportive, conflicted, and controlling. The support component measures the family's openness, team spirit, shared interests, and activities; the conflict component measures the family's conflict and lack of support and organization; and the controlling component measures the use of rules as well as religious and achievement expectations that maintain family stability (Kronenberger and Meyer 2001).

One of the diagnoses to be reviewed in this book is avoidant/restrictive food intake disorder (DSM-5) formerly known as feeding disorder of infancy (FDI). It is prevalent in approximately 4 percent of the general population and accounts for 2–3 percent of all pediatric hospital admissions. This diagnosis is given to children under the age of six, and typically the symptoms occur between three and twenty-four months of age (Kronenberger and Meyer 2001).

"Feeding disorder of infancy or early childhood is a syndrome characterized by a failure to eat adequately prior to the age of six, causing weight stagnation or weight loss" (Kronenberger and Meyer 2001, p. 307).

Children with avoidant/restrictive food intake disorder/ FDI may meet the criteria of nonorganic failure to thrive as well as of reactive attachment disorder. The characteristics of avoidant/restrictive food intake/FDI are most apparent during feeding; the child will often spit out food, push the food away, refuse to open his or her mouth, scream, and turn his or her head away from the food. The parent often responds with frustration and tries to force the child to eat, which may cause the child to equate eating with unpleasantness.

Children with slow-to-warm-up temperaments make up most of the children diagnosed with avoidant/restrictive food intake disorder/FDI coupled with a family environment that is plagued with chaos, neglect, or conflict, which may cause the child to become upset and suppress the child's appetite. There are higher incidences of attachment problems in children with avoidant/restrictive food intake disorder/FDI than in healthy children, and troubled marriages are often revealed in children with avoidant/restrictive food intake disorder/FDI (Kronenberger and Meyer 2001).

Another diagnosis category found in children is somatoform disorders according to the DSM-IV, now known as somatic symptom and related disorders according to the DSM-5. The diagnoses that fall under the category of somatic symptom and related disorders all share the common feature of "the prominence of somatic symptoms associated with significant distress and impairment." (DSM-5 p. 309) Due to individuals with somatic disorders presenting with physical pain and discomfort they usually initially engage in treatment with their primary care physician or possibly an emergency service facility versus a mental health professional.

The updated classification in the DSM-5 defines the major diagnosis, somatic symptom disorder, based on positive symptoms (distressing somatic symptoms plus abnormal thoughts, feelings, and behaviors in response to these symptoms). However, medically unexplained symptoms remain a key feature in conversion disorder and other specified somatic symptom and related disorder. Children with somatic disorders are typically present with headaches, stomach aches, nausea, and fatigue.

Family emotional distress is listed as a commonality in children diagnosed with somatic disorders. In addition, the somatic disorder may co-occur with anxiety and/or depression. If the anxiety and/or depression is in response to a major life event such as parents separating or divorcing, the child is typically diagnosed with an adjustment disorder.

The emphasis on the emotional health and well-being of the family cannot be ignored when assessing children. Selective mutism is yet another childhood disorder that has a strong connection to the family environment or family dynamics. Selective mutism is a disorder in which a child does not speak in one or more common situations such as school or to strangers.

In many cases of selective mutism, conflict and marital disharmony are often cited. Mothers of children diagnosed with selective mutism have been described as lonely, anxious, deprived, and depressed; and harbors resentment toward the child's father, and often enmeshed with the child. This enmeshment may cause the child to avoid interaction with others to demonstrate his or her loyalty to the mother.

On the other hand, the child may resent the enmeshment with the mother and use his or her silence to control her. Furthermore, parents reporting enmeshed relationships with children may have elevated scores on certain scales on the Minnesota Multiphasic Personality Inventory, which is indicative of depression, low self-esteem, alienation, anger, and the need for a symbiotic relationship. Please note that these same parental feelings often succeed divorce.

This leads me to discuss a very challenging topic formerly known as gender identity disorder and now known as gender dysphoria. According to the DSM-5-TR, people with this condition feel that the sex they were assigned at birth does not match the gender with which they identify. The word *dysphoria* is defined as a state of feeling unwell or unhappy

(*Webster's Ninth New Collegiate Dictionary p. 391*). Signs of gender dysphoria may be identified as early as ages two to four. The reasons for gender dysphoria are still being explored. However, it is noted that single mothers of boys who make disparaging remarks about men, specifically when the fathers are detached or absent from the family, may cause confusion regarding what sex their sons may choose to identify with. Why would a boy want to grow up to be what his mother hates? Equally, if a girl has a close relationship with her father and he makes disparaging remarks about women, why would she want to grow up to be what her father hates? In addition, trauma may play a role in gender dysphoria. Again, this is still being explored and may not be completely understood by anyone who hasn't experienced it.

In addition, The Diagnostic and Statistical Manual of Mental Disorders is constantly evolving. As mental health professionals research and gain more knowledge, the manual is updated to reflect the new findings.

One of the most prevalent disorders among our children today is attention-deficit/hyperactivity disorder (ADHD). According to the Centers for Disease Control and Prevention (2022), about 9.8 percent of children between the ages of three and seventeen years old were diagnosed with ADHD from 2016 to 2019. It further suggests that boys are more likely to be diagnosed than girls. Children with ADHD tend to be inattentive, disorganized, restless, impulsive, and hyperactive; these symptoms are disruptive and often create problematic social environments for the children. Attention disorders have two categories: attention deficit disorder (ADD) and ADHD. Children with ADD present with symptoms of lack of attention to details, difficulty sustaining attention, failure to listen, organizational problems, distractibility, failure to complete activities, and forgetfulness. On the other hand, children with ADHD display excessive behavior, squirming, difficulty remaining seated, inappropriate noises and vocalization, and difficulty waiting.

Interestingly, the behaviors described in the diagnosis criteria for ADHD and ADD are often displayed by children of recently divorced parents. As stated previously, divorce accounts for 85 percent of behavioral problems in children, and boys in divorced-mother-headed households tend to display more aggressive, impulsive, and rebellious behaviors than boys in intact families. The adjustment period following a divorce is approximately two years, according to Clapp (1988). There appears to be a direct correlation between

ADHD diagnoses in our youth and the divorce rate, which often leads to a lack of father–child relationships. Further, ADHD often occurs along with conduct disorder (CD) or oppositional-defiant disorder (ODD) in as many as 50 percent of ADHD diagnoses.

CD and ODD are said to be among the most common psychiatric disorders among children and adolescents. The characteristics of CD and ODD are disruptive, disobedient behavior and the breaking of societal norms. Children are diagnosed with ODD much earlier than CD; children with ODD may not develop CD; but children diagnosed with CD were previously diagnosed with ODD in approximately 25–40 percent of the cases. In addition, the diagnosis of CD in children is a predictor of antisocial personality disorder in adults in nearly 50 percent of the cases (Kronenberger and Meyer 2001; American Psychiatric Association 1994).

DSM-5-TR defines ODD as "a recurrent pattern of negativistic, defiant, disobedient, and hostile behavior toward authority figures" (American Psychiatric Association 1994, p. 91). Diagnostically, ODD is characterized by symptoms such as arguing with authorities, refusal to comply with requests, losing one's temper, irritability, externalizing blame for misbehavior, vengeful behavior, annoying and provocative behavior, and appearing angry and resentful (Kronenberger and Meyer 2001, p. 83).

Individuals diagnosed with CD often experience instability in school, on their jobs, with relationships, and in finances; they are at higher risk for chronic substance use; and they typically have a lifelong history of rule-breaking, and law-breaking, behavior (Kronenberger and Meyer 2001). Family and parental dysfunction are detrimental for children diagnosed with ODD and CD. Some research findings suggest that preschoolers with ODD demonstrate problems with security attachment and separation anxiety, and children with CD often have histories of negative parent–child interactions. Further, studies indicate that attachment disruptions and social deprivation—such as extended separation from the parent, multiple caretakers, marital conflicts, and poor childcare—predict later antisocial behavior. As a result of extended separation from the parent, the child has difficulty developing loyalty to rules and social relationships because this was not fostered by the child's role models or attachment figures (Kronenberger and Meyer 2001).

The above information indicates that disruption of attachment, reduced parental attention, and inconsistent parenting seem to be factors in children with CD. These same factors are also noted in divorced families. Divorced households or single-headed households often have inconsistent supervision and lack rules, which are also known to contribute to CD and ODD. Children of divorced parents often feel detached from their fathers as well as reduced or, quite often, no attention from the father following the divorce. To gain attention, these children escalate their negative behavior, and parents sometimes unintentionally reward the negative behavior, which in essence reinforces it.

For example, a child may ask to talk to or see his or her father, but the mother says no. The child then responds by crying or throwing a tantrum; the father is then called as an agent to discipline or settle the child down; and the child learns that if he or she acts out, the negative behavior will get the father's attention.

To address some of these behaviors, family treatment programs started being introduced in the 1960s as parent management training, behavioral parent training, or parent training. In addition, a growing trend in the United States is mandatory parenting classes for parents going through a divorce. My concern is for the many children who are born into a single-parent household whose parents may not be getting this much-needed information. Furthermore, how much follow-up is done to make sure the tools that are taught to effectively co-parent are being implemented? Another concern is that classes are not required in every state; in some states, the decision on whether parenting classes are mandated for divorcing parents is left to the individual counties.

CHAPTER 9

The Power of the Father

We cannot deny the power of the father and the impact his presence or his absence has on his children. The presence of both parents is needed in children's lives.

Other factors related to single-family households, according to the US Department of Justice, are that children in these environments are more likely to have behavioral problems because they tend to lack economic security and adequate time with parents. The *Journal of Research in Crime and Delinquency* (1997) reports that "fatherless families are the most reliable indicator of violent crime in a community." The report also suggests that more drug use, gang affiliation, and school expulsions are also higher in fatherless families.

The US Census Bureau report (2020) cited a research project completed by *Pew Research Center in 2019* indicating about 23 percent of children in the United States are living with one parent, which is an estimated 19 million children living in single parent households. According to the US Census Bureau (2022) there are 10.9 million one-parent families with a child under 18. In 1968 when these statistics first became available, 13 percent of children were in single-family households.

My questions are these: Are we living in a changing world because of our changing family dynamic? Is our changing family dynamic negatively impacting children? What can we do as a nation to get back on track and give the children of this nation the best possible opportunities to be successful?

I understand that not every person makes a good parent. Children are better off living with one healthy parent than living in a toxic family environment. Many issues impact how well children fare without a relationship with the noncustodial parent, such as the relationships the children have with extended family members. Are there positive role models in the extended family who provide support for the children? Positive and negative educators and coaches both have an impact, and interactions with neighbors and family friends can play a positive or negative role in the lives of children. In addition, members of clergy and the church "family" can play a vital role in impacting children.

In the perfect world, we would live in a society where everyone loved one another, demonstrated mutual respect, and protected children at all costs. Unfortunately, that is not our world, and children who do not have good family structures or other supports fall prey to things that no child should ever have to endure.

No child should ever feel alone or unloved. Regardless of what happens to their parents' relationship, at a minimum, children should know that they have the love and support of their parents.

If you as a parent don't take responsibility for saying positive things to your children, you leave them open for the world to tell them who they are, what they can become, and what they can do with their lives. There is power in the spoken word. Children need to be loved and encouraged. If they are struggling with things, we don't call them bad, stupid, or tell them they will never amount to anything.

What message are you sending to your children? If you are a parent and you make the choice to be absent, you are sending a message. It may not be the message you want to send, but there is a message. Your child is left to try to figure out why you chose to be absent, and their interpretation can include thinking that you don't love them, you wish they were never born, or you don't care what happens to them.

If parents don't provide children with love, support, and encouragement and God is not a part of their lives, someone will fill that space. And the message they are given will be what they believe.

We are living in a time of urgency with our children. It is imperative that parents examine themselves. If you need to make changes to be a better person and a better parent, then do that. If you don't think you are worth changing for—although you are—please consider the importance to your child. Be a positive parent who speaks life to your children so that they will grow up knowing that they are loved, supported, and encouraged. Regardless of what is happening in this world, you can increase their confidence to believe that they can accomplish anything that they want to accomplish.

As stated at the beginning of this book, I am not a parent, but I was a child of parents who divorced. I knew what I needed and wanted from them. Fortunately for me, I got it. I had two parents who apparently fell out of love with each other, but it didn't have anything to do with me or my brothers. We continued to know that our parents loved us and would be there for us no matter what was happening in our lives or their lives. I knew I had two safe homes that I could be in because I still had two parents who loved me more than whatever differences they had with each other. Yes, it takes a level of maturity, and you must both have emotional intelligence to make it happen; but you do it because your child is worth it.

It is my prayer and hope that every couple who has a child together can live happily ever after and rear their children together in a home full of love. However, that is not what always happens; people fall out of love, things happen in relationships, and couples decide that they cannot move forward together. But before you let go, make sure you have truly done everything you could to make your marriage or relationship work. Once you have and you believe that divorcing or separating is the best way to move forward, don't forget that your children still need both of you.

The next section of the book shares stories of single parents, two single moms and a single father. The single father also shares his story of never meeting his biological father and how that impacted his life. They discuss co-parenting issues and the impact those issues had or still have on their children.

This portion of the book is based on real events, but certain details, places, and characters' names have been fictionalized or left out. The focus of this section of the book is to understand the perspectives of single parents concerning issues they have faced and the impact they believe those issues have had on their children.

CHAPTER 10

Gabriella's Story

Gabriella reports that, while growing up, she never thought about moving out of her parents' home. She always wanted to be a mom; even as a teenager, she never thought about what she wanted to be professionally. She thought about getting married, living in a nice home, and having children.

She stated that she never thought she was going to be a single mom but found herself in that situation at the age of eighteen. Unfortunately, she had to end the relationship with her son's father because it was unhealthy. Gabriella reflected on the lack of involvement of her son's father but expressed gratitude for how her siblings and other extended family members were there to support her and her son.

After a few years of not dating, she reconnected with an old friend. They became romantically involved, and she got pregnant with her second son. The boy's father was relocated to another state for his job. He didn't pursue visitation with their son, but he provided financially for about four or five years.

Gabriella's experiences with dating and being a single mom fueled her to start dreaming of a future of her own, including going to college, establishing herself in a career, and purchasing a home for her and her sons.

She began making plans and taking the necessary steps to move forward in her life in a positive manner. She decided on the university she wanted to attend, applied, and was accepted. The problem was that this university would require her to move to another state, away from her family support.

However, she was determined to make a better life for herself and her children. She did exactly that, against all the odds, and went on to pursue her dreams.

She excelled in all her classes, and her professors marveled at her level of intelligence. She graduated from college, started working in her profession, and ended up meeting her Mr. Right. They got married after dating for a few years. He became the father figure for her children, and they had more children together; her husband never drew a distinction between her sons and their younger siblings.

However, she believes that both of her sons have a sense of loss and lack of family structure and history. Gabriella shared that neither of her sons had developed a relationship with their biological fathers and at this point they are not interested in having a relationship with them. She feels that her sons may have felt and thought, *Why am I not good enough to be loved?*

She indicated that she tried to do everything she could for her sons. Gabriella may have overcompensated because of their absent fathers and at times let them get away with things they shouldn't have.

She fondly talked about activities she would do with her sons. She made sure they had structure, spent quality time with each of them, and made sure they knew that she loved them.

She shared some of the challenges her sons had while growing up and some behavioral issues, especially as teenagers, but as adults they are doing well.

CHAPTER 11

Jade's Story

Growing up, Jade always knew she was going to college; she never had a second thought about higher education. She started off wanting to be a teacher because of the impact that some teachers had on her life. She was torn between doing what she wanted to do and pursuing what her parents wanted her to pursue. Right after graduating from high school, Jade went to college, participated in sports while there, and graduated on schedule with her bachelor's degree.

Jade was full of ambition and knew that what she wanted to do in life would require a graduate degree, so she applied for grad school. After completing her graduate degree at age twenty-six, she hoped to find a position in her home state but didn't receive any suitable offers.

She did land a position right after graduation, but she had

to relocate. Jade was bold and fearless and went to another place that was new for her to continue pursuing her goals.

Her life was not looking exactly how she planned, but it was certainly moving in the right direction. She was meeting new people, navigating through her new city, and genuinely enjoying her life.

And yes, after about a year or two, she met a potential significant other, and they began to date. She had her education and professional life handled. She was taking on professional roles that many people at her place of employment thought would be too much for her, but she proved them all wrong.

However, her next assignment caught her off guard. After dating someone for two or three years, she learned that she was pregnant with her first child. She fondly reflected on the experience of telling her dad. She expected it to be a difficult conversation, but when she told him, he was happy and said it was about time that she gave him a grandbaby.

Although she struggled with the reality of becoming a single mother—something that was not part of her plan—she is grateful for having her daughter. She feels that having her daughter made her a better person.

Jade made every effort to make her relationship work

with her daughter's father, but she considered him to be noncommittal and ultimately ended the relationship.

After the breakup, she focused on being a good mom, and advancing her career. The advancement led her to relocate to another state. She welcomed the fresh start in a new city, a new home, and a new job.

Jade and her daughter's father had a schedule for visits, and that initially worked very well. She finally became ready to date again. After a couple of years with one man, her boyfriend proposed, and they got married.

From that point on, co-parenting was difficult. She described parenting with her daughter's father as "tumultuous." He soon relocated to another state because of his career, and that eliminated his visits with their daughter for a period.

Jade and her first husband were married for several years and had a daughter together. Her husband was a good father not just to their daughter but also to her oldest daughter. Unfortunately, due to infidelity, their marriage didn't last, and Jade found herself a single mom once again.

Her ex-husband remained an active, involved dad. However, he became distant and inconsistent when Jade decided to move on with her life and date again after being single for a few years.

Jade remarried, but that marriage didn't last due to her new husband's drinking problem. She didn't want that behavior around her daughters.

When asked, "How are your daughters' relationships with their fathers, and how are they being impacted by their relationships with their fathers?" she stated, "That makes me want to cry because I know I played a part in it. I made choices in dating and getting married that negatively impacted my girls, and that bothers me." Unfortunately, no mother can protect her children from the emotional pain caused by fathers who choose to be absent or inconsistent.

Jade said she feels that the inconsistencies of her daughters' fathers have left them wondering,

Why am I not good enough? What is wrong with me?

Jade indicated that both of her daughters have articulated how the lack of relationships with their fathers has impacted them emotionally and in their own dating lives. However, they both have graduated from high school, her oldest daughter has her bachelor's degree, and her youngest daughter is in college pursuing her degree.

CHAPTER 12

Jax's Story

Jax initially didn't realize that there was anything different about his family. His mother was and is an amazing mom, and he has a big brother. His mother made sure they had what they needed, and his brother took care of him and watched over him. He wouldn't allow anyone to do anything to Jax and was always there for him.

His mother met his "real dad" when he was five or six, and they got married when he was ten or eleven. They have been together ever since.

Jax reflected on wanting to reach out to his biological father, whom he refers to as his "donor." He had a couple of questions for him: "Why didn't you want to get to know me?" and "What happened so badly between you and my mom that you chose not to take care of me?"

I would add, "Who would choose not to be there for this child or any child?"

Jax stated, "My mom told me she never discouraged my biological dad from having a relationship with me, but she wasn't going to chase him down and try to force him to have a relationship with me either."

He sent a letter to his father when he was about twelve, but it went unanswered. He decided at that time to quit trying.

However, now an adult and a father himself, he decided to try once again. He and his father had a brief conversation that never amounted to their developing a relationship.

He said, "What was hurtful was learning that he had other children and ... that he is there for them but not me." Jax reported at the time of this interview that he still has never met his biological father and that he has accepted that now.

Jax went on to talk about his own journey in fatherhood. He is the father of two. Becoming a father wasn't planned, but he has been there for his children and will always be there for them.

He said that he and his children's mother are no longer together, but they co-parent. Jax processed some of the initial challenges they had, but over time they were able to work things out.

He stated, "I know my children have a lot of questions about what happened between me and their mother. They're old enough to see a lot on their own now, but I tell them that I will answer all their questions when they are eighteen." He indicated that one question they will not have is, "Where is my dad?"

He proudly talks about his children's academic and athletic accomplishments. It was so refreshing talking to Jax. He exemplifies what fatherhood should be in every way. Jax is proof that the status of a father's relationship with his child's mother doesn't matter. Do what is necessary, like Jax, to make sure you are fulfilling your role as a father.

CHAPTER 13

Additional Risks for Children in Single-Parent Homes

Earlier, I discussed some of the mental health concerns in children following a divorce or separation. There are other risks too, according to my interviews with a school psychologist and a retired county magistrate of domestic relations.

The Story of Ms. C, School Psychologist

Ms. C is in her third year as a psychologist in the school system. During our conversation, it was obvious that she genuinely cares about the children she serves and wants them to be successful. For a person who works in the school system, regardless of how much they care, the outcomes can be inauspicious without parents working with them to support and guide their children.

She stated it is challenging to get parents on the same page as it pertains to getting services for children. She reported that the school staff struggles to get parents together for meetings to discuss the needs and recommendations for children to be successful in school.

Ms. C discussed being able to identify whether children have spent time with their mom, dad, aunt, or a grandparent based on their behavior when they return to school after a weekend or a break. She said that most of the children she provides services for are typically with their mothers, grandmothers, or aunts and that only about 30 to 40 percent of the fathers are engaged.

Sadly, 20–25 percent of the students on her caseload are involved with children services. In these cases, grandparents often act as the legal guardians. The grandparents try to include the mothers in meetings, but they rarely engage and the fathers in these cases are absent.

During the week, Ms. C can work with students and provide tools that allow them to be successful during the week, but once they return home, they must do what is necessary to function in their environments.

She works with her students on executive functioning and social skills. She stated emotional disturbance takes precedence over social maladjustment when securing services for students. In addition, children are often more concerned with eating and being in a safe place than they are with their school performance. Ironically, it is their academics that could make the difference in establishing a better life for themselves in the future.

She tries to engage parents all year, the therapists reach out and teachers reach out, but parents push back when the school staff discuss special education. Some parents wait until the end of the school year to contact the school because only then have they realized that their children are failing all their classes.

Ms. C works in a primary building with children in grades five through eight. On average, these students are three grade levels behind their same-age peers.

Not all students need special education, but many need some support for progress monitoring, such as an Evaluation Team Report, which is the step before an Individualized Education Plan (IEP) is created. Both services require the consent of the custodial parent, both parents, or a guardian. The goal of students on IEPs is to eventually graduate from them by learning and implementing new tools that will improve their classroom performance.

Another problem being faced by the schools is truancy. Unfortunately, courts get involved due to parents' not making sure that their children get to school. In some cases, children don't attend school all year.

In my conversation with Ms. C, I had these questions:

- How is it possible for a child under the age of eighteen not to attend school all year?
- Where are the parents when it is time to attend a meeting to discuss their children's school progress?
- What is happening to these children who lack their parents' support?
- If these parents aren't making sure their children are attending school, what else are these children lacking?

Next, I interviewed Charlita Anderson-White, BS, JD, MBA, a retired Domestic Relations Court Magistrate.

During Ms. White's career, she spent three years serving as a legal aide, five years as a prosecutor in juvenile court, and twenty-three years as a magistrate in domestic relations court. She became emotional when processing some of the cases over the years. It was clear during her interview that she wanted to make a positive impact on the lives of the people, especially the youth, who entered her court.

Ms. White reported seeing generations of families—grandparents, parents, and their children as teenagers—all come through her court. She saw grandparents as young as thirty-five and young single mothers having more children. Ms. White indicated that, when young ladies are expecting, they get a lot of attention, but after the child is born, they often feel alone. She believes that sense of loneliness leads them to have another child, possibly to regain attention.

In her experience working in the courts, a large proportion of youth coming through the court had one parent, usually the mother, engaged as support. She said this may have been because the other parent was working and not able to attend, or perhaps they were simply absent from the child's life.

She further indicated that some issues are systemic to children of color, including having court-appointed lawyers, a lack of information regarding resources needed for services such as mental health evaluations, and not being referred to treatment that could mitigate the legal consequences. Unfortunately, not having access to resources can kick off a cycle of youth reoffending or having problems with adhering to probation requirements.

I am certain that Ms. White has touched many lives and will continue to do so in her new endeavor as the Founder and Chief Administrative Officer of the Outside Circle Theatre Project. Her organization was established in 2023 with the intent to "encourage, nurture, and champion works focused on history, social justice, diversity, equity, and inclusion discussions. OCTP gives women and girls an opportunity to express themselves in their own words in a safe, non-judgmental, and inclusive space." Ms. White's organization will surely be a tremendous asset to the community.

CHAPTER 14

Stronger Together

If we take an honest look at the structure of families and issues facing our children, we cannot deny that we are stronger together. Again, I don't condone anyone staying in dysfunctional, unhealthy, toxic, or abusive relationships for children to have both parents. We all know that living in chaos is not good for anyone.

But once someone becomes a parent, that comes with responsibility. Not taking that responsibility seriously, as you have seen in this book and more than likely in some of your own experiences, negatively impacts the lives, self-worth, and overall success of children.

We cannot continue the current trajectory. It is time to take an honest assessment of ourselves, our families, and our communities.

Are we satisfied with our children going to school and

being concerned about their safety? Are we satisfied with our children struggling with mental health? Are we satisfied with our children feeling unloved and struggling with self-esteem? Are we satisfied with our children being involved in the legal system? If not, we must all do our part to be active, loving parents; active, loving family members; and active, loving community members. We need to return to our spiritual foundation and build strong, healthy families and communities. I am still a believer that it takes a village to rear a child. However, if the village isn't there, parents must be.

Finally, my hope is that, if you are not good together as a couple, you will work on communication as parents and have mutual respect to co-parent effectively. In other words, learn "The Dance."

My uncle Joe and aunt LaRue dancing

Dr. Marva, author, dancing

REFERENCES

American Psychiatric Association. 2013 and 2022. *Diagnostic and Statistical Manual of Mental Disorders* (DSM-5 2013 and DSM-5-TR 2022), Washington, DC and London, England: American Psychiatric Publishing

Blackwell, Roger D., Paul W. Miniard, and James F. Engel. 2001. *Consumer Behavior,* 9th ed. Mason, OH: South-Western, a division of Thomson Learning

Carter, Betty and Monica McGoldrick. 1989. *The Changing Family Life Cycle: A Framework for Family Therapy,* 2nd ed. Boston, MA: Allyn and Bacon

Centers for Disease Control and Prevention. (Feb. 25, 2022) *"Mental Health Surveillance Among Children – United States"* https:www.cdc.gov/nchs/nhis

Clapp, Genevieve. 1988. *Child Study Research.* Lexington, MA/Toronto: Lexington Books D.C. Health and Company

Donofrio, Brian and Robert Emery. "Parental Divorce or Separation and Children's Mental Health." *World Psychiatry National Library of Medicine* (Feb. 18, 2019) 100-101

Hingst, Ann Godley. "Children and Divorce: The Child's View." *Journal of Clinical Child Psychology* Volume 10 (issue 3): (1981): 161-164.

Holy Bible, New International Version. 1996. *The NIV Rainbow Study Bible*, Grand Rapids, MI: Zondervan Bible Publishers

Kronenberger, William G. and Robert G. Meyer. 2001. *The Child Clinician's Handbook, 2nd ed.* Needham Heights, MA: Allyn & Bacon A Pearson Education Company

Myers, David G. 2002. *Exploring Psychology,* 5th ed. New York, NY: Worth Publishers

NIV Compact Dictionary of the Bible. 1989. Grand Rapids, MI: Zondervan Bible Publishers

Pew Research December 12, 2019. "About one-third of U.S. Children are Living with An Unmarried Parent" from https://pewrsr.ch/2Fm1q01

U.S. Census Bureau, 2020. *"America's Families and Living Arrangements"* https://www.census.gov

U.S. Census Bureau, 2022. *Mothers Maintain 80% of Single-Parent Family Groups*. November 17, 2022. Press Release Number: CB22-TPS.99 https://www.census.gov/data/datasets/time~series/demo/cps/cps~asec.html

U.S. Department of Justice, 1997. "Single-Parent Families Cause Juvenile Crime" (From Juvenile Crime: Opposing Viewpoints. 62-66 NCJ Number 167319 & 167327

Webster's Collegiate Dictionary. 1991. Springfield, MA: Merriam-Webster Inc. Publishers.

Zucco, Tom. "Divorced Dads Often Lose Contact with Their Children" *Tampa Bay Times*: (Feb. 7, 1996)

Printed in the United States
by Baker & Taylor Publisher Services